OOGLY ES SIN

The Lamentable Ballad of Anthony Payne
Cornish Giant

Alan M. Kent

OOGLY ES SIN

The Lamentable Ballad of Anthony Payne
Cornish Giant

Francis
Boutle
Publishers

First published by Francis Boutle Publishers
272 Alexandra Park Road
London N22 7BG
Tel/Fax: +44 (0)20 8889 7744
Email: info@francisboutle.co.uk
www.francisboutle.co.uk

ISBN 978 1 903427 38 5

Printed by Leopard Print Ltd

For Deano

Preface

In 1975, when I was eight years old my teacher Mrs Metters arranged for Foxhole Primary School to visit the Royal Institution of Cornwall Museum in Truro. On looking around the museum I was instantly struck by Sir Godfrey Kneller's painting of Anthony Payne, 'The Cornish Giant'. Over the years, I had been back to the museum, researching and writing, and often the giant had looked down upon me.

Late one night in 2007 a bleary-eyed discussion took place in the Hawkins' Arms, Probus, with the actor Dean Nolan. Dean was the only performer I knew who could step convincingly into the 'g'eat' shoes of Anthony Payne and we spent the next three months working intensively, researching, improvising and devising a dramatic monologue that would not only convincingly record Payne's life, but be relevant to the twenty-first century. It's a tall story indeed, but I hope I have done the big man justice.

Alan M. Kent
Lanbrebois/Probus
2007

The first professional production was given on 27 April 2007 at the Comrades' Club, Probus, Truro by BishBashBosh Productions followed by a three week tour of Cornwall.

ANTHONY PAYNE – Dean Nolan.

Music by Dalla.

Directed by David Mears and Alan M. Kent.

Designed by John Voogd.

OOGLY ES SIN

Music: Cornish. Traditional: 'The Three Knights'. Lights up.

A three-quarter sized stool, box, candles and sack pre-set centre stage. Payne enters carrying a staff (his halberd) and singing gently to himself. Lights candles. Music fades into:

PAYNE   Pelea era why moaz, moz, fettow, teag,
Gen agaz bedgeth gwin, ha agaz blew mellyn?
Mi a moaz tha'n venton, sarra wheag
Rag delkiow sevi gwra muzi teag.

[Where are you going pretty fair maid,
With your white face and your yellow hair?
I'm going to the well, sweet sir,
for strawberry leaves make maids fair.]

What you buggers lookin' at?

Pause

Eh!?

Pause

Ebm' you never seen anyone built like a brick-shithouse before?
Obviously not. You're all probably from over the River Tamar anyway. Rich buggers with more money than sense. 'Ave a good look at 'ee all – puffed up like bladders of lard.
And you – what you gakin' at boy?
I knaw I ain't no oil paintin' – but you'mmmm oogly es sin.

Pause

That's what the maids up Stratton used to say 'bout me. Oogly ... es ... sin. Charmin'. [*Beat*] They only had a bit of time fur me when I wuz in church of a Sunday, and they'd say, "Anthony, An-thony boy, will 'ee read a psalm from the Bible fur we? You got a voice like an angel ... well, a bench-end angel playing a bagpipe. But a bleddy clear bagpipe at that – and not too much of a drone. They cud hear 'ee up Morwenstow, sweeter than a nightingale, and louder than Farmer Tregaskis' bull on heat. Oogly es sin, but fair boy on the Bible.
'Es – fair boy on the Bible.

5

Pause

Can 'ee see how oi'm a man built too tall fur this world?
Too tall an', well, a bit wide in the waistline. 'Tis a wisht job.
They'm who's short, well, back Bude way, we d'say, they go by
the ground. Well, look at moi nuddack, tidn' zactly next to the
ground is ut? Some days I do go round with me 'ead in the
clouds – especially up on the moory ground, when the fog's
down. I got t'always watch what I'm doin' or sometimes I
d'clank me crown on Sir Beville's Grenville's g'eat coach-
door. I'm in 'is service, see.
I mean, how does it feel to be huge in a world set on being
small? Tell me that, my beauties. That's the question fur all ov
'ee. Fur zertain, they out there, are all small minded. Small
brained. Small beliefs. And tiny pizzles. [*Beat*] Small bleddy
ceilings in here ent there? I nearnly scat me head 'gainst the
durn of the door when I walked in here. Have you seen some
of the plaaces here in [*location of performance*]? I tell 'ee
what . . . they wuz built fur a bunch of pussivantin' pygmies
you'd find in the far h'off H'indies.

Pause

Caw – pardon me, me 'andsomes. Hear of me goin' on. I abm'
even introduced myself. You'll have heard ov me. Most people
have. Well, you can't really miss me can 'ee? I'm Anthony
Payne – professional Cornish giant – or thas' what they d'call
me in the rags. But then they dun't knaw nothun'.
Yes, I'm colossal.
Herculian.
Monstrous.
Enormous.
Huge.
Large.
Prodigious (bleddy hell, thas' a fancy word!).
Vast in the ass.
How tall were you, when you were twenty one? Me – I wuz
already seven foot, two inches. Took a twenty-five boot. Ha – I
got feet like spades and hands like shovels. I got a beauty of
a . . . so the maids d'say. [*Beat*]

Pause

Perhaps I shouldn't be worried, if you d'find me strange. I

6

come from up Budehaven way. Stratton t'be exact. Thas' that bit of Cornwall that nobody d'knaw much about. 'Es – 'tis a bit isolated, an' naw mistake. Some d'say that's why oi'm a bit of a freak. The blood-lines a bit tight. See, they say the apple dun't fall very far from the tree, an' well, mother and father wuz cousins – boath ov 'em big boned. You'm joke, but we Cornish are all cousins. Oi'm probably related to you missus. Y'knaw second cousin removed from your half-sister's brother... When I popped out ov mother, in the year of our Lord sixteen hundred and twelve, the nursemaid said 'twas like a 'uge narwhale washed up on a beach. Granfer said 'twas more like a scene from the bal over Wheal Gwindra, with twenty boys from the core ready with shovels t'hoick me out from the rockface. No-est way! Time they give me a wash and wrapped me in linen, they'd downed a full hogshead ov ale. They edn' seen nothun' like ut. "Big boy inna'?" they went.

Father wuz a tenant farmer with quite a temper on 'un. "Boy," he used to say, "'Eave that big fat ass ov yours up top field, an' bring in the herd."

No-est way, says I, but if I didn' do ut there and then, ee'd give my ear a good ol' scat. I tell 'ee, 'twas good preparation fur what I've 'ad t'put up with.

So what wuz ut like growin' up big?

I 'spect all ov you been teased at one point – an' first of all, yes, you'd called ut most lamentable. I used t'come home taissy as a snake – squalling and screechin', an' nawse dribbling like a barrel ov hay.

[*Childish voice*] "Payne by name, and pain by nature!" the other childer used t'say when I didn' fit in, when I couldn' do it right, when it needed a tiny hand, an' not one o'these 'ere huge Cornish shovels.

"Look after that chield ov yers," people used t'say t'father. "Chield?! Caw d'hell, 'ee idn' naw chield. 'Ee's near bout taller than me now. Anthony wuz born a man, not a boy..."

Sticks and stones, thas' what I say, an' my bones are bigger than anyone's else's t'break. Do you knaw, they used t' push me around when I first came to schooling? I never hurted 'em back though. I'd frame up to 'um sometimes, but I wudn' do anything.

7

You learn not t'say anything . . . You knaw what I mean. But then I started t'think 'bout ut, an' realised it didn' matter t'all. We'm all different ent us? You can't odds the way you turn out. 'Tis natural as the sun rising over Stratton church each morn. Now, I don't knaw much about how the body works – I leave that t'physicians and other marvellous men – but I do knaw 'tis in the blood. I'm certain they who d'work with phials and chemicals – they there alchemists – will learn ov ut one day – but now, well 'tis in the safe hands ov the Lord. Mother did used t'worry an' fret though. See in the schoolroom, we all wore black jerkins, and fur shenanigans, my school-friends had good cause to borrow my back. Well, see how ut d'look like a g'eat blackboard? They'd do that, rather than write on slate. Aw yes, often wuz the time I'd come home with chalked sums and arithmetic on me back. It got so even the master might use me occasionally. "Turn around Master Payne," 'ee'd go. "I've need of a board . . ."

No-est way, says I. I ent no scribble-chack.

Mother d'put spit t'cloth and rub it out, but tell 'ee truth, I liked ut really. Do 'ee knaw? They called me Uncle Tony. Thas' the Cornish fur 'ee. They d'call anyone kindly enough uncle or aunty, s'long as they treat 'ee proper. So, it got t' the point in me schooling where anything excessive would be compared t'me. Time or two, the length of a pitch or game would be marked 'as long as Tony Payne's foot'. So, by and by, I became a story, a living, breathing – ahem – 'epic' story.

Pause

I used t'call my playmates my kittens. Yes – kittens. Well, they were that small compared to me see. 'Es – fur fun, I'd pick 'um up – one under each arm an' take 'um out over to the cliffs. "Show us the world Tony," they'd cry. And that I would. By the arrish on my chin, off we would trek, goin' fur ut like skeiner; me gruffin' and gruntin' like a boar pig an' they grizzlin' up happy as can be. I tell 'ee, I wuz like their own private carriage.

People would wave at we.

"Hey – Anthony – y'g'eat big pook of turf. Where 'ee off now boy?"

Over cliffs, I'd say.

8

"That Payne," they'd say. "He be tough as ling . . . an' d'go furn' like a long dog."

No-est way. I ent no fish or hound, I'd say back, face glowering up.

My kittens loved ut – well, 'til we got t'the edge of the cliff an' I dangled 'um over. They wudn' s'keen then on seeing the world upside-down – I remember now how they roared when I held by their ankles over the ocean. But I would never have dropped them. No, never. Oh – we had some rory-tory rigs back then.

See, we giants are actually quite gentle . . . unless 'tis a rattle-cum-skit ov a rusty Roundhead.

Pause

See, I walk in a land of giants.

Did you knaw that?

This part of the world's famous for we larger-than-life characters . . . Father wuz always tellin' the tales from years gone by. Said how 'is father used t' tell them to him. Heard of Gogmagog have you? Well, backalong, he wuz a famous giant . . . bit like me. Had a beauty of a wrasslin' match with some boy called Corineus up on Plymouth Hoe. They say you'n still see the jaws and teeth of the giant in the Citadel.

Then there were the giants on the Mount of St Michael – or as father'd say in the old tongue – *Carreg luz en kuz*. That giant, he went by the name ov Cormoran, and 'ee had a baissly missus who went by the name o' Cormelian. Hard as nails she wuz. In fact, thas' how the mount got built – by her carrying the rocks out to sea in her towzer.

See, there wuz giants all over the place back then. We wuz normal. 'Twas you buggers who wuz the weird shortarses. There's the legend of Holiburn way down Carn Galva, then there's Trebiggan by the Land's End. Then there's the story of Tom and the Giant Blunderbuss. [*Excited*] In that see, Tom d'kill the giant! [*Beat*] Oh . . . It – er – dun't quite appeal like it used to . . . what with the giant being deaded.

But there's more. Oh – you'll hear it all: The Giant's Chair, The Lady Giant's Chair, The Giant Ralph of Portreath, The Giant of Morval, Ordulph of Tavistock, The Giant Bolster. See, we d'live 'mongst 'em still my beauties.

9

An' then Sir Beville taught me some stories too. We had a glance through his library one day. Showed me this from Havilan's Architrenium (whatever the diggins that is):

Grand theatrical delivery:

"Of Titan's monstrous race (thas' me, fur you'n see I am a Titan – oogly – but a Titan nonetheless ...)
Raw hides they wore for clothes, their drink wuz blood (well, in my case – that's the blood of them cakey Parliamentarians ...)
Rocks were their dining-rooms, their prey their food (personally, I dun't go much on rocks fur dining rooms – they ent very comfortable – but there 'tis ... Personally, I d'like a good-sized table, knife and fork an' so on ...)
Caverns their lodging, and their bed their grove, Their cup some hollow trunk."
Hollow trunk! What do a mean hollow trunk?
Well, I suppose my room at Sir Beville's is a bit of cavern, and the bed is ... well, big ... king-sized ... I suppose you might say a bit ov a hollow trunk.

Pause

I tell 'ee what – they'll 'ave some trouble getting me out ov there when I 'ang up me 'alberd. Sir Beville wuz just joking to me if I die up there they'd have t'cut a hole in the ceiling an' lower me down with block and tackle.
What for Sir? I asked ov 'un.
"Why man, it would be impossible to bring you down the stairs no matter how many men we might have to assist ..."
Sir Beville had a point. I must admit, I near 'bout have t'bend over double t'get up there. Least the ceilings up there edn' a bad height ... Most other plaaces I have t'be hunched over. I tell 'ee, 'tis like living in a doll's house.
So, you all knaw a bit more about me now dun't 'ee?
See, I ent s'scary as I look, am I?
Oogly I may be ... but oogly of heart I'm not ...

Pause

Now, 'av I told yew lot the tale of me an' the log-laden ass ...
Bugger, I'd better say donkey – seeing as how we'm in polite

company. I'n picture it right now. You've ne'er seen such actions.

'Twas the Yuletide – and Sir Beville had all the house fires lit. You'n imagine ut can't 'ee? 'Es – cold enough t'freeze yer . . . Well, 'twas brass monkeys fur certain. We had icicles on icicles I tell 'ee, an' the beef, well the beef in the larder wuz s'frozen you cudn' cut ut with a wood-axe. Anyway, my lady looked inta the hall on Christmas Eve, and the fire there wuz properly languishing. There wuz no logs in the grate basket neither, and she wuz shivering good an' proper. Boy Diggory wuz sent out inta the snaw t'fetch more wood.

Well, 'tis no good sending a boy when 'tis surely a man's job. Ent that right boys?

Now, Diggory took his own ass (er . . . donkey) wid'un, t'carry the logs homeward. Horses – now I can handle they, but asses – they'm a different matter altogether. 'Bout as much sense as a carrot half-scraped. Well, the morning must've gone, because by noon, her ladyship come in t'see me. "Anthony, the boy has not returned with the wood for the fire . . ."

(She d'speak cut up like that – but she's a good old maid).

Really my Lady Grace, says I.

"Would you be as so good as to see if you can find him?"

She wuz some clip with me, her.

Course I will my lady, says I.

Anyway – out I goes inta the snaw, and stank down towards Rattenbury Woods, where the aglets and gribbles d'graw in the bottoms. Course, I find 'un right away.

"'Ee wun't move fur love ner money," says the boy Diggory, pointin' to his ass – er – donkey. "I d'think 'ee's frozen solid."

No-est way, says I. No ass gets frozen.

Now, unlike some, that boy, 'ee d'speak proper broad, so I ad a hard job t'ear 'un properly, what with the snaw and wind howlin'.

Thing wuz – ol' donkey didn' look very happy, you. Boy Diggory 'ad piled 'un up with enough logs fer you t'build a house with. His legs wuz near bout breakin' under the strain ov ut all.

Ee-or, went the ass, actin' up some silly.

Shut up I said, but the ass wudn' shut up.

Ee-or.

No-est way ass.

Ee-or, he went, an' kept on braying away like there wudn' naw tomorra'.

Some row that wuz. You could near 'bout hear 'un up in Deb'n. I told 'un t'hush his bal.

Ee-or, he went again.

Some yip on yer ass, I said t'boy Diggory.

"He always been like that," said the boy. "Full o' himself. A proper knaw-all 'ee is fur an ass."

Well, I wudn' havin' naw knaw-all fur an ass make a fool o' me. Do 'ee knaw what I did?

I didn' worry nothun' 'bout un. I just picked up the ass an' 'eaved 'un an' all the wood on top of me shoulders. 'Twas a proper game o'coose t'start with – donkey totally begritcht my actions and wuz bedolin' and belving like no tommora', scritchin' and scuffin' at me. Ears an' tail everywhere 'twas. Young boy's jaw dropped and he wuz nearnly 'bout frozen t'the spot. It didn' weight much – honest. Ass on me – and a way to go!

Ee-or, went the ass.

"Dun't'ee cab that donkey any," went the boy to me, worried in the face.

Dun't be s'cakey. Course I wun't cab 'un any, I said.

Ee-or, went the ass, trying t'kick me cheens a bit'; his head in me clunker all the way up the hill.

'Ee wuz lookin' at me some funny.

What you looking at ass? I said to 'un.

If he could speak, I reckon he might've said, "You – ye g'eat thick giant. What on earth are 'ee doing carrying me – a log-laden ass on a winter's day. I must be some hinderment to 'ee."

Can't odds ut ass, I said to 'un. My lady is in need of wood fur her fire.

"Ebm' you got anything better t'do? Like being a useless good-fur-nothun' giant."

No, says I. I serve my lady the best I can.

Said the ass, "I'm in need of some good, dry oats . . . an' a carrot or two."

Now that ass didn't like ut much on top of my shoulders. 'Ee struggled and 'ee shook and 'ee kicked and 'ee wriggled like an angleditch, but I wudn' having none of it (I tellee' 'twas good training for later 'gainst they donkey-donged Roundheads). My g'eat footsteps were goin' deep in the snaw with the weight of the ass on my shoulders – boy followin' on – not really knawing what to do, but I s'pose quite amazed at what wuz goin' on. Well, when I stepped through the drang of gate, I shouted out I wuz back. 'Twas dummets by now, and the rest of Sir Beville's boys thought me mazed as a curlew. I didn' care. I just walked on inta the hall and gently let down the ass. I untied his legs and let un go gallivantin' around the hall. Ee-or, he went, and then her ladyship comed in, all dressed up t'the nines in furs and woollens. 'Twas that cold, you could see her breath still. She wuz carryin' a bussa of warmed ale, which went down a treat. You might say she wuz somewhat surprised to see an ass frolicking around the place, but she didn' say a pile.

"Ass and fardel!" I shouted quick as a flash. "Ass and fardel for my lady's yule."

An' that night, the fires burned bright. Plenty of goodness in that timber. Lady Grace thanked me an' the boy. An' do you knaw what . . . we felt so sorry fur that ass, we kept 'un inside, and give 'un a few good, dry oats fur his trouble. He cluckied down in the corner, on the planching. From then on, me an' that ass got on like a house on fire. I wudn' 'bout to have no more dog-dancing from 'ee!

Pause

'Es – they wuz the good times. You never knaw it then – so be mindful yourselves – realise what you have now. Don't long for tomorrow and dun't think of yesterday. Think of the now. Be happy with what you've got. Giant advice that is.

See, great and sudden change wuz on its way, and many lamentable events were about to fall over the happy halls of Stowe. Whacks of change and dissolution were in the air, with the King and his parliament in fatal strife. You could see months before that 'twas goin' t'be all out war for the land. I had one place only – and that wuz right next to my master – by Sir Beville's side. All through the handsome hills and vizzy

13

valleys of Cornwall went the cry, "Grenville's up!" and many a noble knight and yeoman turned northwards toward Stowe. I saw the mounted messengers ride to and fro. It seemed as if the whole world wuz descending on our little village. Overnight, small suddenly turned large.
Strange and stalwart faces began to arrive to claim a place in our ranks. Diddies Lane wuz filled with pike-men, and Bridge Street groaned with the wheels of newly-forged cannons. Retainers were enrolled day and night, and the smooth sward of the bowling green and Fawn's paddock were dented by the hoofs of horses, and the tread of serried men.
My job? Aside from professional 'Cornish Giant'? Well, foremost, I wuz bodyguard to my master. Part of this role though, wuz levying the mimsy men from the western mines. 'Course they sort o' tom-toddying tinners are always full of piss and vinegar, thinking that they got the world hold ov by the asshole. Tighter than a gnat's ass they were. And short with it.
"Why must us pay the levy Mr Payne?" said one boy to me. "Tidn' our war be it?"
To fund Sir Beville's campaign, I said – lookin' un straight in the eye. Got a problem with that ave' 'ee?
I gived 'un a look that would scare old Nick himself. 'Ee wudn' 'bout t'mess with a stuggy sod like me, so on he strammed.
"No Mr Payne. Not a problem at all," said the boy, payin' up quick. They wudn' happy though – not really, these underground men – and they walked away talkin' like lawyers chitterin' on 'bout Stannary rights an' all.
Bugger yer Stannary rights, said I. Dunnee' knaw there's a war on.
Each day I wuz stagged out with work, sweatin' like a poultice, running around, giving our arms and rations, to the mixed multitude all there for 'the king and the land'. Stowe wuz no longer my childhood home. It became a garrison surrounded by a camp. All order wuz scat t'lerraps. I tried to keep up morale handing around nicies and nubbies, but I tell 'ee, you could sense the fear . . .
The way wuz no-est.
All peace wuz strubbed out.

Lights dim

At last, on the morning of 14th May, tidings arrived that the battalions of parliament, led by Lord Stamford, were on their way northwards, and not many miles off t'all. Now, Stamford, t'my' mind, I allays pictured 'un dressed up like an 'oss marine – an' naw use t'man nor beast. They called we Cornish so many hurtful names – Robbing choughs and the King's pixies, and the like, thrawing it all up to we. They handed out pamphlets to all they met on the way to Stowe – to rubbish my master's name. Yeow! – that d'make moi' blood boil. Still, the army marched from Stowe in the cold dark hours of the dawn two days later. I wuz proudly there by Sir Grenville' side, sat on my cob Samson. A good horse – an' a lot more sense than an ass . . . I mean, donkey . . .

We were joined by Sir Ralph Hopton and in total, the army numbered two thousand four hundred on foot, with five hundred on horse. The odds didn' look good though. We wuz outnumbered two to one.

Knawin' this, we kept low in the dark, deep in the vearns and vuzz, while Hopton divided our army into four columns. The enemy were encamped on top of the hill. In short, our plan wuz t'sneek up on the buggers at five in the morning. Thas' when it all kicked off though – our boys who stroathed sneakily up the hill were seen by the sentries, so in came the close volleys. Meanwhile, our footmen were pressing four ways up the hill towards the enemy, while the enemy wuz obstinately endeavouring to keep them down. I tell 'ee straight – a good eight hours this went on for, and our crew wuz runnin' out of ammunition and heart. Thas' when the pussivantin' parliamentarians levelled their pikes, and ran down the hill at we. They slammed in hard an' fast. Loose yer footin' an' you'm doomed.

[Breathless] My Lord Grenville wuz bowled over in the rush, so I let Samsom go an' picked 'ee up under one arm, an' grabbed a pike with the other.

You party's goin' t'pay fur that, I said.

In faith, I turned proper oogly.

I'n move fast with a pike mind – like poetry in motion.

15

Moast ov they roundheads avoided me, but yaffuls ov 'um I
wrassled. They went down like winnards.
I tell 'ee, I wuz fierce as a buckrat, an' quicker than duckshit.
Any of the leading ranks I smashed inta and broke their
pikestaffs in two. Well, despite moi efforts, t'be honest, the
roundheads wuz gainin' the upper hand. That wuz 'til Sir
John Berkeley's musketeers comed in, an' fired away. That put
they inta a rout an' so we pushed 'um up the hill again. The
zam-zoodled enemy were gradually giving away, an' started to
leave possession of their cannons and their dead.
At last, by late afternoon, the commanders of all four Royalist
columns met. In ground near the brow of the hill, where
having joyfully embraced one another, they pursued their
victory, recovering the top of the hill, which the emmetty
enemy had a-quitted. Thas' when our cavalry comed in, an'
finished 'um off. They slowered up an' retreated off the field.
Do 'ee knaw, we took 1,700 prisoners that day? I wuz in jerks
all evening, like a pig pissing.
We all named ut Stamford Hill after the loser. Master
Grenville returned home to Stowe that night, to rest, and plan
the next campaign, but I stayed on the battlefield to help bury
the dead.

Pause

I tell 'ee – 'tis really a most lamentable thing, picking up the
bodies of dead.

Pause

Much harder than donkeys I tell 'ee. Dead men dun't grunt
and bray – but their silence is chilling.

Pause

It do go right through to your bones and stay there for days.
No-est way, says I to me.
I had the moaning mimby miners from the west dig large
trenches. When these were laid open, they could hold ten
bodies side-by-side. So we carried down the slain and placed
them gently in. I had them bury any roundheads too. Men
who've fought deserve dignity is my way ov seeing ov ut.
We had nine of ours laid in one of the costeens and I wuz
bringin' down another tucked under me arm – a man by the
name of Jakka Bray. I'd knawed 'un fur years. When I'd picked

16

'un up, 'ee didn' have much t'say – being dead I thought – but suddenly 'ee began yippin' up t'me, "Surely you wouldn't bury me Mr Payne, before I am dead?"
I tell thee, man, says I, our trench wuz dug for ten, and there's nine in already. You must take your place.
"But I bean't dead," says Bray, looking a like tooth-drawer.
You'm meant for there, says I.
"I haven't done living yet. Be merciful Mr Payne. Don't ye bury a poor fellow into the earth before his time."
I won't hurry thee, says I. I mean to put thee down quietly and cover thee up, and then thou canst die at thy leisure.
Boy Bray looked at me like I wuz mad. But I wudn'.
See, my purpose here wuz kinder than my speech. I 'ad 'un a beauty there!!! [*Laughs*]
That is often the way with me as you'll knaw by now. I carried 'un carefully back to his cottage not far off, and charged his wife to stem the flow of blood from his wounds. I'm happy to say that 'ee lived and his children now flourish in the parish. So that trench, well, it only carried nine . . . One more of we, is one less ov they in my view.
[*Sighing*] Now you may think we walked home from the battlefield, happy as larks that we'd won, that wudn' the case t'all. War d'do terrible things to a man's mind. I cudn' sleep that night, even though I'd had double my normal stoop of wine. We may 'ave won the battle but the war wudn' over – not by a long chalk. I went downstairs to find Sir Beville pacing back an' forth in the drawing room. He looked like a right pattic.
What are 'ee thinking sir? I asked ov 'un.
"Gentle Tony," he said, "You fought today like a bear . . . So many lives you saved on our side – including my own – I am truly thankful for all ye do."
No need fur it master, says I. I have sworn on my life to protect you, ever since I came into your retinue. Sir – will you read this?
"What is it?"
'Tis only but a short treatise sir, but it says what we achieved today.
So Sir Beville read it: "In this place, the army of the rebels

17

under the command of the Earl of Stamford received a single
overthrow by the valor of Sir Beville Grenville and the
Cornish army on Tuesday the 16th May 1643 . . . Where
should it go?"
Somewhere in Stratton, sir, says I. So leastways if we never
win again, there's one date which we might be proud of.
"Tony, the Cornish have not won many wars, but we shall
mark this."
Come sir, I says, you must be getting rest.
'Twas time to climb the timbern hill.
I could see the cherks of tiredness in his eyes. The war effort
had slowered 'un up lately. He looked thin as a griddle, and if I
only knew what lamentable events would take plaace later
that year, I might have spent a few minutes longer with him
that night. O calamity! Alas, time's a tricky master – always
ready t'prick 'ee like a goad.

Pause

So 'twas inta England we went.
Tidn' a plaace I like much. Do you?
Too many gidgees and glidder, and not enough gew and
gumption.
Thas' my take on ut.
We had long days of riding – an' moast of the boys walkin'.
They bleddy underground men with me, still moaning and
mutting on 'bout this an' tha'. 'Twas July – summer-time, you.
Even so, it ented ut down all the way, the tracks full ov flosh
and flaws, dull and dummaty weather through Somerset. I
looked like a bundle of straw tied in the middle, all kitted up
with armour, an' t'be honest with 'ee, though I wuz in charge
of towing the cannons, I felt like a cow handlin' a musket.
Knaw that feelin' do 'ee? Tidn' good is ut? My mind felt boiled
to jowds time we got t' Lansdown.
But Sir Beville wuz all, "Mr Payne, stay with the dragoons . . .
That is where I wish you to be."
And I wuz all, but sir, but sir, but 'ee didn' want to hear.
The hill there ent far from the fair town of Bath. I tell 'ee what
– time we got there, I wuz some lampered up with dirt.
Could've done with a tub of water t'soak meself in. No such
luxury fur we, though. See, Sir William Waller – commander

18

of the Parliament's Western Association forces – controlled all
this area. 'Spect 'ee wuz walkin' round like a turkey, bossin' 'is
boys about. He'd hung his coat 'pon Cromwell a long time ago.
Sir Ralph – always healthy as a trout – and Sir Beville had just
received additional troops from the King, so we reckoned on
having four thousand on foot, two thousand on horse and
three hundred dragoons. Waller, we reckoned, lacked the
number we had . . .
Aw – there wuz some fartin' around t'begin with – skirmishes
an' the like. But they had the ground see . . . an' when they
bleddy roundheads charged down the slope, it put we buggers
into retreat. You cudn' odds ut. 'Twas a bold move by they. We
rallied though – especially they on foot.
I stayed on Samson an' went steamin' inta the fray.
Take that y'lubbercock!
Have a taste of Tony's dreadful dag!
We'm on you, y'vile wagel!
No-est way, y'whitneck!
Thas' got you, y'grooted goat!
I'll split your heads in two like a pair of mazzards.
Have some ov that y'jowstering jigger!
You boy – y'ruzzin' roundhead! See that vugg there – thas'
your grave . . .
Whack.
Scat.
Huel.
Gopher.
Clang.
Scollucks.
Spal.
Spuke.
Scranch.
Scrow.
Shig.
Skeat.
Slock.
Smulk.
Smudder.
Slooge.

Sputter.

Squinch.

Stram.

Stave.

Strake.

Stickled... [*Beat*]

Stubbed... [*Beat*]

Sweeled... [*Beat*]

Swoggled... [*Beat*]

Stuggied.

Phew!

Got the bugger!

The battle raged on back and forth across the hedges of Lansdown. Outnumbered and outflanked, gradually the Parliament's army gave ground to we. We 'ad a breather – fur we wuz all proper knacked. There wuz an aim to repeat the success of Stamford Hill. Sir Beville and his pikemen tore inta the enemy fire till they gained the brow of the hill. 'Twas the bravest thing I ever saw, fur they received all the enemy's small shot and cannon. Grenville and I stood firm 'gainst any rout. Twice we withstood charges from Sir Arthur Hesilrige's horses, but alas, under the third assault many of our Cornish boys were deaded – and among them my lord... good Sir Beville... It wuz a shot that another day perchance should have hit me. Shoulder to shoulder we stood...

Now the air wuz so darkened by the smoke of powder that for ten minutes there wuz no light seen. Only the volleys of shot gave bursts of fire. This, my beauties, wuz the greatest storm I ever saw – and it caused in me the greatest storm of my heart. Samson, my 'oss, had two or three musket balls in him, which made him tremble under me, and I could hardly with my spurs keep him from lying down. Eventually he came to lay down, and if I'd had the strength, I'd have carried 'ee back to Stowe too.

When the smoke cleared, there wuz Sir Beville, split in two – like a piece of haven driftwood.

"Take care of Grace and John good Tony," he mouthed softly to me. And then he wuz gone – a giant amongst men felled like an oak tree.

Within minutes Lansdown wuz over – save for a sudden final volley of musket fire. The roundheads slinked away and we were left to count our dead. Several hundred had gone to meet the Lord that day. Success at Stamford Hill wuz an age away. I gained another horse and placed Sir Beville upon him, and then set forth back to the west. See what I said earlier came true – time's a tricky master – always ready t'prick 'ee like goad. Then I had to write to her Ladyship. I took best quill and parchment, and set me down at an inn.
Suddenly I wudn' too tall fur this world no more:

[*Reads*] Honoured Madam. Ill news flieth apace. The heavy tidings no doubt had already travelled to Stowe that we have lost our blessed master by the enemy's advantage. You must not, dear lady, grieve too much for your noble spouse. You know, as we all believe, that his soul was in heaven before his bones were cold. He fell, as he did often tell us he wished to die, in the great Stuart cause, for his country and his king. He delivered to me his last commands, and with such tender words for you and for his children as are not to be set down with my poor pen, but must come to your ears upon my best heart's breath. Master John, when I mounted him on his father's horse, rode him into the war like a young prince, as he is, and our men followed him with the swords drawn and with tears in their eyes. They did say they would kill a rebel for every hair of Sir Beville's beard. But I bade them remember their good master's word when he wiped his sword after Stamford fight; how he said, when their cry was, "Stab and Slay!" "Halt! men; God will avenge". I am coming down with the mournfullest most lamentable load that ever a poor servant did bear, to bring the great heart that is cold to Kilkhampton vault. O! my lady, how shall I ever brook your weeping face? But I will be trothful to the living and to the dead. These, honoured Madam, from thy saddest, truest Servant, Anthony Payne.

Pause

I led his son, Sir John, back to Stowe where there were great lamentations indeed. Her ladyship's love wuz gone inta the earth.

But then, times d'riggle an' you d'start t'live with a hisk ov' hope in your heart. Between that time and 1660, I served Sir John well, and became as fond of him as my old master. The Restoration served me well. All around Cornwall again there was hope, buoyed on by the new King's letter of thanks. Sir John had been a helpful higgler in the return of the King to the throne and he received from Charles g'eat sums of money, offices and the earldom of Bath. Among other plaaces of trust, 'ee wuz appointed Governor of the Garrison of Plymouth. So down the Tamar we rowed, to the old town of Devonport. I tell 'ee straight – what transpired there, came as quite a shock to me. It wuz the day of my forty-eighth birthday, when Sir John invited me into his quarters. What adventures next, I wondered, as I stood before him.

"Anthony," he said, showing me the Royal seal. "I have a letter from the King. You know how high you are held in his esteem. He wishes you to be appointed Halberdier of the Guns here at Plymouth. Will you accept, he wonders?"

Course I'll accept sir, says I, s'long as I can go back to Stowe from time to time.

"I don't see that as a problem. I'll write back to him this instant . . . There is something else though –"

"Sir?" says I.

"The King has commanded the court artist – one Godfrey Kneller – to arrive here, in order to paint a portrait of you. 'Tis to be in your natural presentment."

What, me sir? But oi'm proper oogly! I mean, you or your mother, p'rhaps – but me?

"The King being a tall man, An-thony, sees something of him in you I think . . . The artist arrives next week."

So thaas' how I became a painting. Yeah – me, prinked-up in a painting!?

Days it took fur this here growdering Godfrey fella to get me right. Have you ever had t'stand still for hours on end? It d'play hell with yer back I tell 'ee, and this here feeble-voiced Godfrey wuz all, "Just a little more to the right Mr Payne" and then "Could you lift you head slightly luvvie? You're beginning to droop . . ." The only way I could get through it

22

wuz t'every-so-often have a sup of my allowance of wine.
The sun wuz streaming in through the window of his studio.
Do you think I'm oogly as sin? I asked Godfrey that morning.
"Mr Payne – you are as beautiful a specimen of humanity as I
have ever had leave to put to canvas."
Can 'ee just make sure me thighs idn' too big, I asked ov 'un.
I'm awful conscious of how big me thighs are . . .
"I am a truthful artist Mr Payne . . . but we shall see what the
brush strokes can do."
So there I am, boobed up on the wall. Tidn' a bad likeness I
must admit. I'm nor sure about the outfit. Red idn' zactly my
colour really. He painted me with my right hand on a cannon
and my left holding the tall halberd denoting my office. I
dun't spect 'twill last, but there 'tis.
"There Mr Payne," said that gabbling Godfrey, "you are a
work of art."
No-est way.

Pause

One more tale I should relay. Not of art, but of artfulness. I am
an old man now, in my seventies. Gigantic still, but not quite
so strong. Still Halberdier though. Still in the service of Sir
John Grenville. Scribblers and scratchers came to talk me
about my life. Even the London papers ran stories about 'The
Giant of Cornwall'.
Time d'move quick see.
Lady Grace passed on, and King Charles and James. William
and Mary wuz enthroned, but new days wuz coming. There
wuz devotion now to the Head of Hanover. New lines, new
kings.
For a laugh, on the day of the anniversary of when the old
King wuz beheaded, my ranks had me ordered a calf's head,
served up in a 'William and Mary dish' of delf crockery. Now
to me, this wuz pure mockery of the beheaded King and all
that I believed. They knew I wuz a Stuart man.
What's that? says I.
"In honor of the most lamentable beheading of King
Charles," says they, laughing.
With one move, I picked up the g'eat grubbling dish and
threw it out of the window. I pity anyone below, who'd find

calf-head, dish and vegetables rainin' upon them. No matter –
I wudn' about t'have any ov they yank my halberd.
So I didn' just take one ov 'um on.
I took on the whole lot.
'Es – wrassled the buggers around the ramparts. You ebm' seen
nothun' like ut. There wuz bodies goin' everywhere. They
didn't knaw the strength ov a sebmty-seven-year-old man.
Have 'ee seen muscles like these afore?
Come on, then, says I. Let's hitch. Have a go if you think
you'm man enough fur a giant.
"A'right," says they.
Fee fi fo fum, says I fur ricks. You'll wish your cake dough.
"An you'm a full weight without the wrapper."
Remember says I, fair play is good play.
"Scrollocks t'that," says they.
Tung! We'm on a hitch from hell.
First the fore hip, then the crook.
Then, the fore crook.
Then, the back crook.
Move forwards.
Jiggle a bit.
Try t'catch 'un when he ent looking.
Fore Heave.
Back heave.
Under-heave.
Scat 'un back.
Then the heel.
Back Step.
Back Strap.
Pull 'un over the hip inta' a lock arm.
Cramp 'un out.
Pull under and heel.
Get 'un inta' a double sprag.
Right, no sticklers here. Room fur a cross collar. Knuckles on
the throat. Crowbar hitch. Slip out of the jerkin. Thaas' the
way.
Then, t'top ut all – the flying mare. Whumpf!
The last one who took me on – well, bit of a larrakin 'ee wuz.
Strong as an ox too. By now, I'd seen the joke. After all, I'd

been a joker moast of my life. 'Twas certain I deserved some lubbins back. I 'ad 'un a beauty. In a crowbar, then a fore crook. Then 'twas time fur the Payne Special – right in the scrollocks.
'Eaved 'un off the rampart straight inta the dung heap. Cockerel there wudn' best pleased, an' neither wuz matey. I stood on top ov the ramparts and shouted down to 'un, hey – boy, there's some sauce fur thy calf's head!

Pause

No-est way! This tall tale is almost done.
And full of sauce an' skull-draggin' it has been . . .
Would 'ee believe ut years back, days an' days ago? Somehow I'd become famous. There wuz ballads in the penny dailies 'bout me. Everyone knew me as the Cornish giant. I could be tall in a small world. Maybe even the world had grown with me – become more tolerant, more sympathetic, more understanding. They'm who knew me didn' see the oogly; they only seen the grace. Sir Grenville. Sir John. Godfrey Kneller. Jackka Bray. Even that log-laden ass of an ass.
That wrassling match at Plymouth – well, in truth, that wuz the last true hitch I wuz t'have. 'Twas the right plaace really, what with that other giant Gogmagog havin' a match there with Corineus, all them centuries ago.
Naw – 'twas time fur me to head home. Back up the Tamar I went. Still waters. The slow lift an' dip of the oars. I found shelter and repose in the very house and chamber where I'd been born. Comfortin' that.
I needed to leave the halberd and the cannon.
I needed to walk the fields and the cliff-tops of Stratton. Smell the sprouncing sea again. Listen to the gorming gulls some more.
I needed peace in a life that had seen too much war. War – now, maake naw mistake: thaas' wha's really oogly. We need it about as much as a toad d'need side-pockets.

Pause

And now you've listened, all ov 'ee d'knaw I ent naw freak ov nature.
I'd always been different. Neither gick nor gack.
Different in size, but different in heart too.

Think about that will 'ee?
One day – my kittens – it'll serve 'ee well.

Pause

Right, I'd best be off...
People to look down to ... [*Beat*]
Places t'bang me head into ... [*Beat*]

Blows out the candle.

Got a bit of a dance to go to ... an' a fine maid in mind ...

Music: 'Helston'. PAYNE begins to dance. His first movements are delicate and traditional, but as the dance continues build in contemporary moves.

Fade out to the faint sound of the music.